CW00658771

A BOOT UP

THE EASTERN PEAK

Roger Redfern

First published in Great Britain in 2011

Copyright text and photographs © 2011 Roger Redfern

British Library Cataloguing-in-Publication Data
A CIP record for this title is available from the British Library

ISBN 978 1 906887 18 6

PiXZ Books
Halsgrove House, Ryelands Industrial Estate,
Bagley Road, Wellington, Somerset TA21 9PZ
Tel: 01823 653777
Fax: 01823 216796
email: sales@halsgrove.com

An imprint of Halstar Ltd, part of the Halsgrove group of companies
Information on all Halsgrove titles is available at: www.halsgrove.com

Printed and bound in China by Toppan Leefung Printing Ltd

Contents

How to use this book

The Area

The eastern fringe of the Peak District National Park has an amazingly broad range of landscapes but is predominantly composed of the Millstone Grit we associate with the Dark Peak towards the west.

Though much of the land dips gently towards the eastern lowlands of South Yorkshire and northern Derbyshire its western frontier has some dramatic scenery, including the famous Eastern Edges overlooking the course of the River Derwent.

The Routes

Very attractive routes, both short and long, can be created in these eastern uplands, including the crest of these Eastern Edges from Derwent Edge in the north to Froggatt Edge and Curbar Edge further south. Some of the most charming country in all Peakland lies in the north-east, valleys like the Porter, Ewden and Bradfield Dale where you will discover peace far from the hotspots further into the National Park.

Each route here is graded from Easy to More Challenging with further details of distance, height ascended and the type of terrain covered, so helping the reader to choose a suitable route. The information blocks contain details of distances and heights in both imperial and metric measures.

All the walks are covered by Ordnance Survey Outdoor Leisure Map 1 - "The Peak District - Dark Peak area" and Ordnance Survey Outdoor Leisure Map 24 - "The Peak District - White Peak area".

The Maps

The maps in this book give only outlines of each route. Reference to an OS map will add interest and help avoid going astray.

Always go well equipped, especially on the routes that involve tough terrain and higher altitude. If unsure of fitness try one of the easier routes first! Not all of the routes described have convenient places providing refreshment so always take some food and drink.

Tell someone where you are going and your expected time of return. And, having checked the weather forecast, only tackle the challenging routes in clear conditions.

Useful websites:
Peak District National Park
www.peakdistrict.gov.uk

Rail travel:
www.nationalrail.co.uk

Peak District Tourist Board
www.visitpeakdistrict.com

Bus travel:
www.transpeak.co.uk

Peak & Northern Footpaths Society
www.peakandnorthern.org.uk

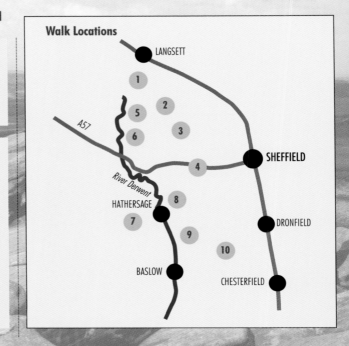

Key to Symbols Used

Level of difficulty:

Easy 🖤

Fair 🖤 🖤

More challenging 🖤 🖤 🖤

Map symbols:

🚗 Park & start

— Road

- - - - - Footpath

● Town

■ Building

+ Church

▲ Summit

🍽 Refreshments

🍺 Pub

Walk Locations

LANGSETT

1

2

5

3

A57

6

4

SHEFFIELD

River Derwent

8

HATHERSAGE

7

9

DRONFIELD

10

BASLOW

CHESTERFIELD

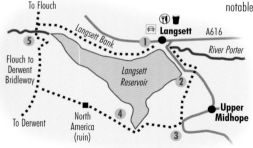

1 Langsett and the Porter Valley

Wild country on the National Park's north-eastern fringe

The Porter or Little Don River flows from the high watershed of the south Pennines more or less south-eastwards into an increasingly deep dale to join the River Don at Deepcar, close to Stocksbridge.

Three reservoirs occupy parts of the dale, adding bright diversity to the open landscape. The elevated wilderness at the head of the dale is notable grouse moor where the summer calls of dunlin and curlew are so often heard. The stone-built village of Langsett makes a very suitable base for the good variety of walking routes possible to create here.

The Midhope Moors to the south of Langsett were chosen for tank training by American forces towards the end of World War Two and evidence of this is still visible. There are concrete roads

Level: 🥾

Length: 3.75 miles (6 kms)

Ascent: 393 feet (120 metres)

Terrain: Tracks and paths around a reservoir.

Park and Start: Langsett Barn car park.

Start ref.: GR 211 004

Info: Information boards at Langsett Barn.

Refreshments: At Bank View Café, Langsett and inn at Langsett.

in the ridge-top village of Upper Midhope and lines of brick ramparts (labelled "Targets" on OS Outdoor Leisure maps).

Here are breezy, wide open moorsides with far ranging views to the highest country of the Dark Peak one way,

and out towards the green and crumpled foothills of South and West Yorkshire in the other direction. These are rewarding walking grounds.

1 From the car park in the plantation south of the A616 road at Langsett walk down past the

Crookland Wood, near Langsett

public house and turn right to cross the impounding wall of Langsett Reservoir using the public road.

2 Beyond the impounding wall the road climbs round a corner beneath trees. Take the first track on the right and walk up beside the plantation on the right to reach the uppermost houses at Upper Midhope village.

Langsett Reservoir - dry weather

Brookhouse Bridge, above Longsett

3 Opposite the first farmhouse on the left take the ancient track that drops a short distance to the public road at a sharp bend. Turn right along Thickwoods Lane - notice the concrete surface dating from its use by military tanks in World War Two.

4 After going down close to the reservoir level the track crosses Thickwoods Brook and climbs to the ruins of North America Farm (notice bullet marks on the stonework from wartime gun practice) and cross Hingcliff Common to join the famous Flouch to Derwent bridleway across the high moors.

5 Turn right (north) and soon drop to Brookhouse Bridge at the head of Langsett Reservoir. Climb a short distance and take the path leading off right (east) which traverses the wooded slope called Langsett Bank to return to the car park starting point.

Crossing the River Porter above Langsett

Langsett Reservoir was the largest one owned by the former Sheffield Water Authority (now part of Yorkshire Water). Construction began in 1898 and was completed in 1904. The valve tower on the impounding wall was modelled on the gateway of Lancaster Castle and the public road running along the top of the dam is the longest dam-top highway in the country. When it was being constructed residents of the district demanded reassurance that the quality of the work on the reservoir "be above suspicion". They were remembering the collapse of the notorious Dale Dike Reservoir in nearby Bradfield Dale in 1864 which caused the loss of 250 lives.

April shower over the Little Don Valley

2 **The Best of Ewden Dale**

A glimpse of a south Pennine gem

The Ewden Beck flows in a deep east-west valley that, like its southern neighbour of Bradfield Dale, has the feel of a true northern declivity. It is a place of secrets, of reservoirs, woods and sweeping moorland horizons. The route suggested here gives a flavour of its charms, more particularly good views from high ground across the dale.

Two large reservoirs lie on the valley floor, fringed by extensive plantations, but from the high ridge to the north we can walk easily and savour the broad vistas in every direction. This is typical hill farming country; stone-walled pastures are juxtaposed with heather moors, attractive farmsteads lurk in sheltered corners and the historic Mortimer Road winds, twists and climbs up and down the dale en route to the market town of Penistone.

Our route begins up at the ridge-top village of Bolsterstone almost one

Level: 🥾 🥾
Length: 5.5 miles (8.75 kms)
Ascent: 790 feet (240 metres)
Terrain: Breezy ridge-top, valley-side paths and public lanes.
Park & start: Bolsterstone village.
Start ref.: GR 271 968
Info: Inn at Bolsterstone.

Map:
The Height ▲
2
The Height
3
Ewden Beck
4
5
Broomhead Hall Cottage
6
■ Wigtwizzle
8
Heads Lane
1
Bolsterstone
7
Broomhead Reservoir

thousand feet above sea level and only a few fields south of the edge of industrial Stocksbridge, but quite out of sight from it.

1 Close to the parish church at Bolsterstone walk west along Heads Lane for almost a mile (1.3 kms) to its end at Hunger Hill Farm.

2 Continue west along the track and go up to the summit of the hill ahead, beyond a few tall conifers. This is The Height, part of Whitwell Moor, and the trig. pillar stands at 1,178 feet (359 metres). A wonderful viewpoint in clear weather.

3 Return down the short distance to the track then continue down it, traversing down the

View east from Whitwell Moor towards Bolsterstone

slope westwards to come out onto Mortimer Road a short distance below Garlic House Farm.

4 Go left down the steepening road, round the sharp hairpin bend and so down to the bridge over

the Ewden Beck and up the other side for another half mile (.75 km).

(5) As the gradient eases look for the first entrance gateway on the left. Go down the drive to Broomhead Hall Cottage and follow the footpath to the left of the buildings and so down and across Broomhead Park to reach Moor Lane close to Wigtwizzle hamlet.

Looking to the Don Valley from Whitwell Moor.

At Waldershaigh, Bolsterstone

Shires near Whitwell Moor

6 Turn left down Allas Lane, cross the head of Broomhead Reservoir on Broomhead Bridge and walk along the road for another third of a mile (.5 km).

7 Just where the Wood Brook comes down through the plantation on the left take the path left that climbs through the trees to come out onto open pastures and go due north up to Heads Lane at the

Broomhead Park from Whitwell Moor

farm buildings associated with the mansion called Waldershaigh.

8 Walk right along Heads Lane back to Bolsterstone.

The ridge-top village of Bolsterstone where this route starts and ends is best known for its Male Voice Choir but long before that was established a castle was built here in the thirteenth century. Part of the stone gateway can be seen to the east of the parish church of St Mary. Pevsner considered these remains to be part of a porter's lodge or guard chamber. Two huge stones lying at the south-east corner of the churchyard may be "lintel stones of a stone circle". The village stocks may possibly have been removed from the castle after it became ruinous. The close proximity of the edge of industrial Stocksbridge to the north does not, happily, spoil the feeling of rurality here at Bolsterstone.

Pike Low summit at the head of Ewden Dale

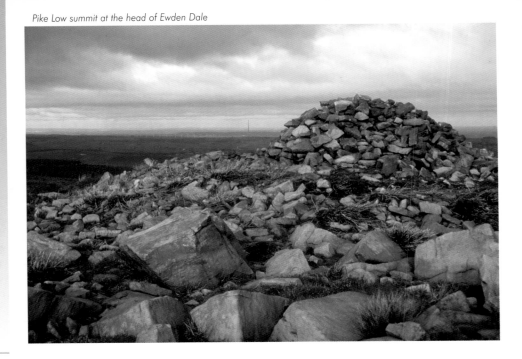

3 **On Foot in Bradfield Dale**

Getting a glimpse of what this lovely valley has to offer

This is the third of the trio of lovely parallel valleys that drop eastwards from the high gritstone moors towards the Don Valley and the north-western outskirts of Sheffield. Some connoisseurs consider the landscape of this deep, green dale the finest in the entire area of the National Park and beyond.

Like the Porter Valley and Ewden Dale this one has the bonus of large reservoirs which add variety and brightness and extra interest. It was the collapse of one of these dams in the mid nineteenth century that caused such loss of life in the lower dale and parts of Sheffield (see more below). Today, though, life in Bradfield Dale is quieter and we can explore moorland,

Level: 🏵 🏵
Length: 4 miles (6.5 kms)
Ascent: 490 feet (150 metres)
Terrain: Steep lanes and footpaths on pasture, some moorland.
Park & start: Low Bradfield.
Start ref.: GR 264 919
Info: Inns at Low and High Bradfield. Café at Low Bradfield. Information at Council Offices. GR 263 917

tilting pastures, dark woodlands and scattered villages to our heart's content. The parish is one of England's largest and the local council have gone to great pains to maintain footpaths and signs.

Agden Reservoir from Agden Rocher

High Bradfield lies at about 918 feet (280 metres) and commands broad prospects up and down the dale. There can be few parish churches with a site finer than St Nicholas, one of the largest in the broad district called Hallamshire.

Choose from dozens of fascinating footpaths, most well signposted. The one described here will, I hope, give you a flavour of what Bradfield Dale has to offer.

1   Start beside the sports field at Low Bradfield and walk up the lane towards High Bradfield. In a few hundred metres turn left on the lane towards Agden Reservoir and opposite the first house on the left take the field path (right) that leads steeply

up to High Bradfield parish church.

 2 Enter the churchyard and walk along beside the battlemented churchyard wall to the churchyard gates. Turn west (left) inside the churchyard to go past the south front and main door of the church and find the path still going west just below the tree-covered motte and bailey fortification called Bailey Hill. Entering the wood follow the path down to the north, cross the Rocher End Brook and go generally north-west across the interesting, toppled ground below the conspicuous gritstone escarpment called Agden Rocher, once a popular climbing ground (less so nowadays).

3 Go through the yard at ruined Rocher Head Farm

Ruins of Rocher Head Farm, High Bradfield

Dale Dike Reservoir, Bradfield Dale

and continue along the farm track to the public road (Smallfield Lane).

(4) Turn left for a very short way to the junction then turn right before taking the footpath on the left side which traverses the rough slope called Agden Side and so descend to the north shore of Agden Reservoir.

(5) Go left (east) on the track beside the reservoir to reach Smallfield Lane again and, just beyond, the hamlet of Smallfield.

(6) Walk along the lane that soon keeps close to the reservoir's edge and return to Low Bradfield.

High summer at Kirk Bridge, Low Bradfield

Of the four large reservoirs on the floor of Bradfield Dale the most famous (and notorious) is Dale Dike. Constructed in 1863–4 it was the first in this valley and in March, 1864 its impounding wall gave way and most of its 700 million gallons capacity thundered down towards Sheffield. A total of 4,511 houses were flooded and 240 persons killed. A new dam was eventually constructed 400 yards upstream of the original one in 1875. A public footpath allows access to the small stones marking the centre line of the collapsed wall at GR 245 918.

Strines Inn at the head of Bradfield Dale

4 **Wyming Brook and Redmires**

A circular route on the National Park's eastern boundary

The three Redmires Reservoirs were some of the first large dams constructed to supply the growing industrial centre of Sheffield (from 1830). They lie at the edge of the broad expanse of Hallam Moors over 1,150 feet (300 metres) above sea level. The smaller pair of Rivelin Reservoirs lie to the north, in the bottom of the Rivelin Valley.

Connecting the two sets of dams is the purpose-built Wyming Brook Drive that curves down from Redmires through what are now mature coniferous woods that look and feel more like something you would find in western Scotland than South Yorkshire. A walk along this broad track or up and down the adjacent boulder-strewn Wyming Brook has been a popular recreation for Sheffielders since Victorian times.

The route described here takes us down, almost to the Drive's junction

Level: ♥
Length: 4.5 miles (7.25 kms)
Ascent: 300 feet (90 metres)
Terrain: Easy paths, some moorland path.
Park & start: Top of Wyming Brook Drive.
Start ref.: GR 269 858
Info: Inn at Lodge Moor, along Redmires Road towards Sheffield.

with the Sheffield to Manchester highway (A57), followed by a path beside the infant River Rivelin, before crossing the heather moor to reach the conduit constructed to conduct water from the headwaters of the River Rivelin around the slope to feed into Upper Redmires Reservoir. An easy walk back along the conduit-side path gives fine views eastwards to Sheffield's lofty western suburbs and a close encounter with a tower built in connection with the Rivelin Water Tunnel (see details below).

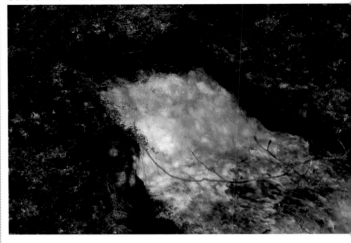

Outlet of Rivelin water tunnel into Rivelin Lower Reservoir

1 Walk north down the length of Wyming Brook Drive for 1.5 miles (2.5 kms) to the second stone bridge (crossing the River Rivelin) just before the drive gains the A57 highway.

2 Take either footpath heading west (upstream) beside either bank of the River Rivelin to reach the footbridge carrying the footpath from Surrey Farm towards the Redmires Conduit.

3 Turn left (south) up the path that climbs gently across the heather moor to the Redmires Conduit.

Oaking Clough feeder reservoir

The Rivelin Water Tunnel was completed in 1910, its purpose to bring 10.5 million gallons of water daily from the Derwent Valley reservoirs to Rivelin for use in Sheffield.

The 6 feet 6 inches high tunnel is 4.5 miles (7.25 kms) long and passes through solid millstone grit, falling to Rivelin at a gradient of 1 in 3600. About 500, 000 gallons of the daily total transported comes from the gritstone layers in the tunnel's western half.
Find the outlet at GR 273866.

4 Turn left to walk eastwards along the conduit-side path all the way to Redmires Road where

Wyming Brook and Redmires

Rivelin Valley from Oaking Clough

Redmires Upper Reservoir

the conduit empties into Upper Redmires Reservoir.

5 Turn left to walk the half mile (.75 km) back to the starting point at the top of Wyming Brook Drive, noticing the carved stone against the wall (right) at GR 261857 which was part of the decoration on the front of the old "Grouse and Trout" Inn which lost its licence in 1915 and became an empty shell in 1934, later completely demolished.

Beside the Redmires Conduit

The Grouse and Trout stone, Redmires

5 Along the Duke of Norfolk's Road

Bar Dike to Fairholmes – a high level linear walk requiring transport

Traversing the high and exposed moorland between the top of Bradfield Dale and

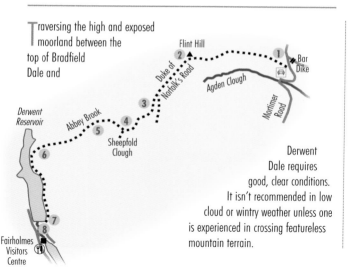

Flint Hill

Duke of Norfolk's Road

Agden Clough

Mortimer Road

Bar Dike

Abbey Brook

Sheepfold Clough

Derwent Reservoir

Fairholmes Visitors Centre

Derwent Dale requires good, clear conditions. It isn't recommended in low cloud or wintry weather unless one is experienced in crossing featureless mountain terrain.

Level: 🥾 🥾 🥾
Length: 8 miles (12.5 kms)
Ascent: 425 feet (130 metres)
Terrain: Moorland paths, steep clough paths and level reservoir track.
Park & start: Bar Dike on Mortimer Road.
Start ref.: GR 246 945
Note: You need to make arrangements to return to your starting point from Fairholmes.
Info: Refreshments, cycle hire and information at Fairholmes Visitors Centre. GR 173 893

That great pioneer rambler and fighter for public access to the moors, G.H.B. Ward, described this route as "the wildest Yorkshire moorland walk south of Wharfedale". We begin where the Mortimer Road climbs out of Agden Clough to reach the moor-top at the pre-historic defence work called Bar Dike.

Easy walking for several miles westwards along the path past Hurkling Edge and Flint Hill. This broad track became a public "road" legalised for ever by an Enclosure Act of 1811 and named in honour of the Duke of Norfolk after he became owner of a vast tract of this upland associated with his country seat at Derwent Hall (now vanished beneath the waters of Ladybower Reservoir).

The descent to Derwent Dale is dramatic, on a narrow path down a narrow ravine with plenty of evidence of former landslips. Our route ends on a level track down the eastern bank of Derwent Reservoir to reach the Visitors Centre at Fairholmes, downstream of this reservoir's mighty masonry dam.

Note that one must arrange some sort of transport back to the starting point at Bar Dike - maybe use two vehicles, one left at each end.

1   At Bar Dike walk west onto the moor, keeping to the footpath along the crest of Hurkling Edge. In about 2 miles (3.25 kms) we gain the barely noticeable slopes of Flint Hill at about 1,542 feet (470 metres).

2   The path now turns to head south-west. In a further mile (1.5 kms) take special care to fork right on the path that leads quite soon to overlook the head of the Abbey Brook.

3   The path keeps to the edge of the steepening drop into the clough. We soon cross Bents Clough with the rugged ground of Berristers Tor across the ravine to the north.

Peat grough in winter, Duke of Norfolk's Road

Looking up Abbey Brook, late summer

In Abbey Brook

The path soon delivers us to the confluence with Sheepfold Clough. There used to be two useful shooting cabins here but they were long since vandalised and removed.

Landslip territory, Abbey Brook

As we head west on the first leg of this route Broomhead Moor lies to our right, fairly much out of our sight. It had the reputation a century ago of being the finest grouse shooting ground in England. The Rimmington Wilsons of Broomhead Hall entertained Edward VII here, among many other famous sportsmen. At a later date Hermann Goering heard of the good sport to be had here and vowed to visit Broomhead – but he never actually made it!
These moors are today popular for their productive bilberry bushes and in August the heather creates a giant emperor's carpet.

5 Follow the improving track as it traverses the slope westwards.

6 In about 1.75 miles (2.8 kms) we come above the first coniferous plantation that heralds Derwent Dale. Continue down through the trees to the main dale-bottom track that we now follow all the way southwards down the east side of Derwent Reservoir.

7 Just beyond the giant impounding wall of the dam take the path that drops to join the tarmac public lane.

8 Turn right along the lane and soon reach Fairholmes Visitors Centre.

Crow Stones Edge overlooks Derwent Dale

6 **Back Tor and the Delights of Derwent Edge**

High views of Derwent Dale from a famous tor-dotted escarpment

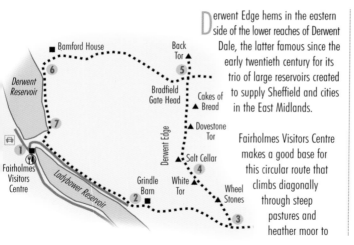

D erwent Edge hems in the eastern side of the lower reaches of Derwent Dale, the latter famous since the early twentieth century for its trio of large reservoirs created to supply Sheffield and cities in the East Midlands.

Fairholmes Visitors Centre makes a good base for this circular route that climbs diagonally through steep pastures and heather moor to

Level: 🥾 🥾 🥾
Length: 8.5 miles (13.5 kms)
Ascent: 985 feet (300 metres)
Terrain: Steep field paths, rough moorland and reservoir-side track.
Park & Start: Fairholmes Visitors Centre.
Start ref: GR 173 893
Info: Refreshments, cycle hire and information at Fairholmes.

reach the watershed of Derwent Edge, notable for its several remarkable gritstone tors. All have appropriate names given by local folk centuries ago - Wheel Stones (alias Coach and Horses), White Tor, Salt Cellar and Cakes of Bread. Our ridge-top wandering culminates at the 1,765 feet (538 metres) summit of Back Tor from where there are magnificent 360 degree views and which the late John Derry, champion of the great outdoors, described as "a fitting region for creatures that love loneliness". Yes, it's a wild, wide place "far from the ways of men".

Retracing our steps a short distance we descend by a long, twisting path, finally through more planted conifers to the banks of Derwent Reservoir for an easy ramble back along the water board track to the starting point. Altogether a varied route that includes hill pasture, open moor-top and reservoir-side.

Grindle Barn from Derwent Edge

1 At Fairholmes Visitors Centre below Derwent Reservoir's imposing impounding wall (GR 173 893) we walk along the public lane that swings round the uppermost reach of Ladybower Reservoir and so past the various surviving dwellings of Derwent village.

2 Just before gaining the mouth of Grindle Clough a path goes up the fields on the left. We climb this, passing restored Grindle Barn and continuing on the track along the top edge of a plantation to come out on the open moor and head up on the path to gain the watershed at about

Grindle Barn in winter

fairly easy to miss. Continue along the ridge to Dovestone Tor and the Cakes of Bread beyond that. Then we gain Bradfield Gate Head, once an important east-west route between the head of Bradfield Dale and Derwent Dale. Soon after this we climb to the top of Back Tor.

5 Return southwards from Back Tor to Bradfield Gate Head and turn right (west) down the path that drops all the way to the reservoir-

The Salt Cellar, Derwent Edge

1,489 feet (454 metres).

3 Turn left (due north) along the watershed to pass close beside the famous Wheel Stones tor, locally known as the Coach and Horses because from certain places in Derwent

Dale it resembles a horse-drawn carriage heading north.

4 There's a gentle ascent past White Tor until we come in sight of the famous Salt Cellar tor, standing to the left of the crest and

The gritstone tors of the Dark Peak were formed in the same way as the tors on Dartmoor. Erosion of the softer rock beds and the surrounding peat has exposed them into often bizarre forms like the ones on Derwent Edge seen at close quarters on the route described here.

Probably the best known in the entire National Park is the isolated Salt Cellar which, incidentally, is more difficult to ascend than it looks (even harder to descend gracefully).

It is very popular as a foreground for photographs looking out over Derwent Dale to the lofty plateaux of Bleaklow and Kinder Scout.

side. On the way down we come close to the ruins of Bamford House, a former keeper's cottage, but turn down steeply instead of passing the ruin.

 Soon we enter Shireowlers South Plantation and so gain the reservoir-side track.

7 It is now simply a matter of walking left (south) back to Fairholmes Visitors Centre.

The Bradfield Moors from Back Tor

Wilfrey's Nield on Wilfrey Edge north of Derwent Edge

In a bid to attract German bombers away from the industrial heart of nearby Sheffield a "decoy city" was set up on the long moorland slope that falls eastwards from the crest of Derwent Edge. Generators and batteries of electric lights were installed and illuminated these moorsides in a hope of distracting the airborne enemy to drop their lethal loads here.

At a later date cables supported on tall pylons were stretched across the Bradfield Dale reservoirs in a bid to prevent German aircraft using "bouncing bombs" to destroy these dams in a copycat reaction to the Allied destruction of German dams in the Ruhr.

Well Head Barn and Derwent Edge

7 Double Crossing of the River Derwent

A mainly valley route in the charming area around Hathersage

Historic Hathersage lies at the lower end of the popular Hope Valley, just above the floor of the green dale where the Derwent flows down from the high moors of the Dark Peak. This is Derbyshire's largest river.

On this route we come face-to-face with ancient hillside halls and get broad views of delightful hill country. The ancient stepping stones lead over the Derwent and allow a climb to Offerton Hall and its adjoining hamlet high on the slopes of the heather moors. Not far away lies Highlow Hall, a fascinating old yeoman farmer's dwelling and, like Offerton, one of the famous "Seven Hathersage Halls" said to have been built in medieval times for the seven sons of the powerful Eyre family — each hall visible from the next one.

Level: ♥ ♥
Length: 5 miles (8 kms)
Ascent: 500 feet (152 metres)
Terrain: Field and woodland paths, lanes and tracks. Some steep slopes.
Park & start: Hathersage village.
Start ref.: GR 232 814
Info: Refreshments in Hathersage.

Map showing: A625, Hathersage, Offerton Hall, Stepping Stones, River Derwent, B6001, Leadmill, Highlow Hall, Hogg Hall, Tor, Bretton Clough, Farm, with numbered waypoints 1–9.

On the way back to Hathersage we walk down the lower reaches of Bretton Clough, a deep, wooded valley which once contained working hill farms; now, though, these are all abandoned. The clough is silent but still a place of natural beauty. After the second crossing of the Derwent — on Leadmill Bridge — the final mile back to our starting point is through level pastures with prospects to the old village ahead.

In Gorse Bank Wood, Hathersage

1 There is a public car park on Oddfellows Road at the centre of Hathersage. A good place to begin this route (GR 232 814). Just beyond the George Hotel on the main road walk right, up the steep Jaggers Lane and immediately beyond the last cottage on the left(in about .25 mile/.4 km)

take the path on the left slantwise down to cross the railway tracks on a pedestrian level crossing and in a few metres reach the main road (A625).

2 Cross the main road to the stile opposite. Go down towards the river and head upstream

through several fields until you reach the famous stepping stones.

3 Cross the Derwent on the stepping stones and continue up the slope ahead, through three pasture fields to reach Offerton Hall.

The Hathersage area has several traditional links with the Robin Hood story. As you walk along the track from Offerton Hall towards Highlow Hall notice a stone stoop (pillar) a few metres above on the right. This is Robin Hood's Stoop, the spot from where the outlaw is supposed to have discharged an arrow that landed in Hathersage churchyard - some feat!

The Stepping Stones, Hathersage

Turn up the lane, zigzagging past Offerton House (on right) and Offerton Hall (on left) and continue along the lane south-eastwards to drop into and climb out of Dunge Clough to gain the Abney road at Highlow Hall.

Turn right on the road for a few metres then go through the gate on the left to drop down the large pasture field in front of Highlow Hall.

Enter Highlow Wood, here at the foot of Bretton Clough, cross the bridge by a footbridge then climb the stile on the left. Continue on the path through the wood to enter the first of four pasture fields (note the spring on the right in this first field).

Cottage garden, Hathersage

7 Walk past Tor Farm and where the farm drive joins the public road turn down left on the good tarmac drive to recently restored Hog Hall. The path goes down the next field to re-cross the brook on a small stone bridge.

8 Fork right up through scattered trees to a cattle grid on the drive to Broadhay Farm. Go right, along the drive to join Abney Lane and go to the B6001 road at Leadmill (Plough Inn opposite). Turn left on the B6001, cross Leadmill Bridge then turn left through the stile immediately beyond Leadmill House.

9 The path gives level walking all the way back to Dore Lane at the lodge to Nether Hall. Go forward

The Derwent flood plain looking to Hathersage

Double Crossing of the River Derwent

(left) to soon pass under the large arch of the railway viaduct and keep the brook to your left as you re-enter Hathersage village.

In Hathersage churchyard Little John's traditional grave stands opposite the south porch of the parish church. It is a popular attraction for visitors. He is said to have lived in a nearby cottage (long since demolished) in his last years, after his adventures with Robin Hood had ended.

Bretton Clough from above Hathersage

8 **The Steep Way to Stanage**

Another circular route based on Hathersage in the Derwent Valley

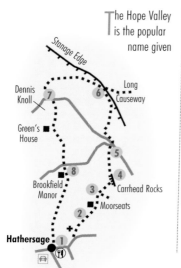

The Hope Valley is the popular name given to part of the Derwent Valley. That part of the lower Hope Valley around the popular village of Hathersage is hemmed in on the eastern side by the long gritstone escarpment of Stanage Edge. The high moors associated with this rock face metamorphose at a lower level to attractive hill pastures, deciduous woods and some coniferous plantation. The V-shaped tributary valley of the Hood Brook opens out to the main valley just where Hathersage has developed.

The route described brings us into close proximity with historic houses

Level: 🥾🥾
Length: 6 miles (9.5 kms)
Ascent: 1,200 feet (365 metres)
Terrain: Field paths, moorsides and high tracks.
Park & start: Hathersage village.
Start ref.: GR 232 814
Info: Refreshments in Hathersage.

like Moorseats, firmly associated with Charlotte Brontë's heroine, Jane Eyre. The churchyard at Hathersage contains the presumed grave of Little John, and the Long Causeway on Stanage Edge was created by the Romans as a safe way across the highest ground here. It later served as a very useful route for pack animals to carry salt and other minerals towards Sheffield and the Don Valley in the east; these pack trains returned with grain for the inhabitants of this generally non-arable area.

1 From the middle of Hathersage walk uphill on the Sheffield Road (A625) and fork left immediately beyond the Hathersage Hall Business Park, along The Dale and opposite the Scotsman's Pack Inn fork left again. We climb the steep lane that soon brings us to the parish church. After looking around the church and its graveyard go out through the lychgate and turn left to the first corner. A stile ahead brings us to rough ground as we keep on this level and so begin a descent ahead.

Moorseats, high above Hathersage

2 Cross the rough pasture surrounded by trees and wilderness hedgerows to discover a fairy tale-like doorway diagonally left. Pass through and climb steeply through the beech trees to eventually reach the site of Moorseats.

3 Walk up the cobbled drive past the house (yes, it is a right of way), through an iron gate and so up past Kimber Court Farm. A stiff climb brings us to an easier gradient. Look for the stile on the left and go through it to open country.

When Charlotte Brontë visited Hathersage in 1845 to stay with her friend Miss Nussey, sister of the vicar of Hathersage, she stayed at the vicarage and was certainly smitten with the ambience of the place. The proximity of wild country and the character of old houses clinging to the surrounding slopes much impressed her.

4 Walk up the moor to the crest of the hill which is the small gritstone escarpment called Carrhead Rocks. Good views.

5 Walk northwards along a small path across Cattis-side Moor to the junction of lanes and take the lane heading north-west for a few tens of metres before turning right up a path that climbs through Stanage Plantation and then slantwise up the steep face of Stanage Edge to join up with the ancient trackway (the Long Causeway) on the breezy top of the escarpment.

6 Walk left down the rutted, stony Long Causeway (made far worse by current use by off-road vehicles) north-westwards and descend in a great curve to the road junction and cattle grid at Dennis Knoll plantation.

The Old Vicarage, Hathersage

Climbers on Goliath's Groove, Stanage Edge

Eyre was the name of an old family of the district and Charlotte Brontë was much influenced in the setting of her best known novel, Jane Eyre, in this very countryside. Moor House, the home of St John Rivers and his sisters, is certainly based upon Moorseats, the old house we pass on the route described here. Mr Rochester's home, Thornfield Hall, is based on North Lees Hall, not far away overlooking the valley of the Hood Brook down which we walk later on this route.

7 Turn left along the lane with the plantation on the right. At the end of the plantation turn right and follow the path down the moor to reach the outlying hamlet which includes Green's House. Turn left through a gate then almost immediately take the stile on the right and go down the fields and through the wood to reach the lane near Bronte Cottage.

(8) Go across the lane and take the path behind Brookfield Manor and so continue south through several pasture fields to reach the end of Baulk Lane which soon returns us to the middle of Hathersage.

Looking across the Hope Valley to Mam Tor

The Plantation, below Stanage Edge

Valley of the Hood Brook, Hathersage

9 **Along Two Eastern Edges**

A flavour of two of Peakland's gritstone escarpments

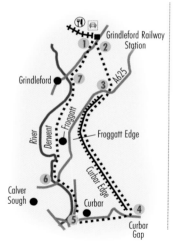

Level: 🥾 🥾
Length: 7 miles (11 kms)
Ascent: 550 feet (167 metres)
Terrain: Woodland, escarpment and riverside paths. Some road walking.
Park & start: Grindleford railway station.
Start ref.: GR 250 788
Info: Refreshments at Grindleford railway station and Calver.

South of the bleak ramparts of Stanage Edge and neighbouring Burbage Edge the next large gritstone escarpments overlooking the Derwent Valley are Froggatt Edge and Curbar Edge. These rear above steep slopes quite dominated by dense deciduous woodland so possess a more benign countenance. Even so their extensive rock faces have many seriously difficult climbing routes on them.

The route described here begins and ends near Grindleford and takes in steep woods, open moor-tops and narrow lanes leading to sheltered valley floor paths. It really is a walking way of contrasts, entirely inside the Peak District National Park with amazingly broad vistas from the tops of Froggatt Edge and Curbar Edge.

1 Start at Grindleford railway station, where trains between Manchester and Sheffield plunge into or emerge from Totley Tunnel. A path starts immediately to the south of the former station building (now a popular café) and climbs steeply to the B6521 road.

2 Cross the B6521 and go straight up Tedgness Road opposite. Where the gradient eases take the footpath forking left ahead (not the one turning back to the left). This path climbs gently behind a large Arts and Crafts house (see detail below) to enter Hay Wood and skirt a National Trust car park. Aim ahead, cross the rocky stream and climb the short distance to the A625 road.

Grindleford station at the mouth of Totley Tunnel

Curbar Edge from near Grindleford

3 Cross the A625 and take the stony track opposite that leads southwards to the crest of Froggatt Edge. Eventually Froggatt Edge becomes Curbar Edge but the scenery remains similar with good views to the west and south-west, over Calver towards Stoney Middleton and the White Peak limestone plateau beyond.

4 Where the hill road from Curbar to Chesterfield climbs to the top of the escarpment at Curbar Gap (car park) turn right, down the road towards Curbar and the Derwent Valley

for a very short distance then take the path on the left that drops straight down near to some old deciduous trees. This path cuts off the hairpin bend on the road. Rejoin the road and walk straight down to Calver Bridge.

Stoney Middleton from Curbar Edge

5 Immediately before the bridge over the River Derwent take the lane on the right and walk north along this until a footpath on the left allows us to walk riverside all the way to the restored weir (originally impounding water for Calver Mill) and the A625 where it crosses on New Bridge.

6 Cross the A625 and continue on the riverside path to Froggatt Bridge. Do not cross the river but head up through Froggatt village, along Spooner Lane and so through fields and woodland to Grindleford Bridge, where the B6521 crosses the Derwent.

7 Walk right up the B6521 and fork left just beyond the Maynard Arms Hotel and so return to Grindleford railway station.

High summer on Curbar Edge

The coming of the Midland Railway route linking Manchester and Sheffield in 1894 meant that villages with a station were now within convenient commuting distance of Sheffield. Grindleford was one of the settlements that saw a spate of residential building developments from this time; mainly of large houses for affluent Sheffield businessmen. One such house is The Gables, skirted by a path followed on the route described here, high above Grindleford railway station, overlooking Tedgness Road. It was built to a design of Sheffield architect Arthur Nunweek in the Arts and Crafts style for the Sheffield factory owner Job Holland and his family in 1912 and remains very much as it was first completed to this day.

On Curbar Edge

Calver Mill

10 **On the Edge of the Moors**

Beautiful valleys on the eastern margin of the National Park

Great areas of the so-called Eastern Moors to the east of the Derwent Valley used to be out-of-bounds to walkers due to a combination of water gathering grounds for the built-up districts further east and jealously guarded grouse moors. Now large parts are owned by the National Park authority and are designated "open country".

Level: 🦋 🦋
Length: 5.75 miles (9.25 kms)
Ascent: 650 feet (200 metres)
Terrain: Moorland track, field and woodland paths, and some road walking.
Park & start: Shillito Plantation.
Start ref.: GR 295 748
Info: Refreshments at Baslow and Barlow villages, not on the actual route.

Here on the edge of Ramsley Moor where the route described starts and finishes we have broad views north into the head of Cordwell Valley, where we are heading, and eastwards across the toppled countryside of north-east Derbyshire, formerly a productive coal mining area. Up here, though, we breathe the fresh, west wind of the high moors and hear the summer song of curlew and skylark.

The great, plantation-covered dome at the head of Cordwell Valley is called Smeekley, literally "smooth cliff". It may look like the giant handiwork of man but is simply the result of erosion over aeons of time of relatively soft shales right on the border of the coal measures and millstone grit.

Further along we climb an ancient lane, then drop to cross Cordwell Valley and go through well farmed land to cross a dark and ancient wood to reach the ancient yeoman farmer's mansion of Barlow Woodseats with its remarkable cruck barn before climbing an ancient bridleway to the lonely hamlet of Moorhall.

1. Start out at the car park at Shillito Plantation (GR 295 748) and walk south to the road junction. Turn right through the gate onto the moor and follow the track north all the way to Car Road.

Godfrey's Cross near Shillito Plantation

2. Turn right, past Smeekley Farm on the right, and in a few metres take a stile on the left and walk through the woodland. Keep right ahead at the obvious junction of paths and leave the woodland.

3. Once out in the field branch left to a stile onto the road.

Be careful crossing the road at this blind bend and use the path directly opposite.

4. Climb the path the short distance to Horsleygate Lane and turn right up it, passing Horsleygate Old Hall (on left). Where the lane becomes level take the stile on the right and go right down through the

Wind bent conifer, Ramsley Moor

caravan park. Once in the next field take the path going across the slope to the right (not over the small stream to the left). After crossing three fields reach the road again.

 Turn right and cross Eweford Bridge then immediately turn

Cordwell Valley which is encountered on this particular route was for a long period the adopted home of the pioneering environmentalist and social reformer Edward Carpenter (1844–1929). As a lecturer in Sheffield's expanding University Extension Movement he came to know this beautiful part of the city's "golden frame".

Towards Holmesfield and Dronfield from Godfrey's Cross

left up Unthank Lane to the scattered hamlet of Unthank.

 At Unthank Lane Farm the road turns sharp right. Just past the farm and neighbouring Rose Cottage a stile on the left (before the bungalow) gives access to the fields.

 Cross the level fields and enter Rose Wood. Fork left down to a tiny brook, climb the opposite bank and leave the wood to cross three more fields and reach the

On the Edge of the Moors

bridleway (Johnnygate Lane) with the imposing seventeenth century house of Barlow Woodseats above the slope.

8 Turn right and follow the bridleway right up to Moorhall hamlet.

9 Turn right on the road which climbs to the top of the hill and continue west, keeping ahead at

Barlow Woodseats Hall

In 1882 Edward Carpenter built a stone cottage set in seven acres at Millthorpe, propounding his philosophy of "three acres and a cow". He wrote several acclaimed books about the environment and on self sufficiency. His modest valley home became a mecca for his admirers, including E.M.Forster, George Bernard Shaw, H.G.Wells and Ramsay MacDonald who could often be seen walking in the the district up to the time of Carpenter's move to Surrey in 1928.

the next two junctions. Shillito Plantation (marked "wood" on most maps) lies directly ahead. We are back at the starting point.

Hilltop Holmesfield from Moorhall